The Let's Talk Library™

Let's Talk About When Your Parent Is in Jail

Maureen K. Wittbold

The Rosen Publishing Group's
PowerKids Press™
New York

Published in 1997 by The Rosen Publishing Group, Inc.
29 East 21st Street, New York, NY 10010

Copyright © 1997 by The Rosen Publishing Group, Inc.

First Edition

Book Design: Erin McKenna

Photo Credits: Cover © Bill Stanton/International Stock; p. 4 © Phyllis Picardi/International Stock; p. 11 © Lou Jones/Image Bank.

Photo Illustrations: pp. 7, 8, 12, 15, 14, 19, 20 by Ira Fox.

Wittbold, Maureen.
    Let's talk about when a parent is in jail / Maureen K. Wittbold.
        p.   cm. — (The let's talk library)
    Includes index.
    Summary: Discusses why jails exist, why people go to jail, and how to deal with having a parent in prison.
    ISBN 0-8239-5043-3
    1. Children of prisoners—United States—Juvenile literature. 2. Prisoners—United States—Family relationships—Juvenile literature. 3. Prisons—United States—Juvenile literature. [1. Prisoners. 2. Prisons.] I. Title. II. Series.
    HV8886.U5W58 1997
    362.7—dc21   96-53427
                                                                                                           CIP
                                                                                                            AC

Manufactured in the United States of America

Table of Contents

What Is a Jail?

Jail is a place where people go to live as **punishment** (PUN-ish-ment) for breaking the law. If you have a parent in jail, you are not alone. Thousands of children just like you have parents in jail. Those kids have many of the same fears, worries, and feelings that you do. Most of all, it is important to remember that it was your parent who broke the law, not you. *You* did nothing wrong.

◄ Someone who is in jail spends time in a cell like this one.

Why People Go to Jail

A person is put in jail when he or she is caught breaking the law. Laws are rules that help to keep peace and order. Laws were created so that people would be treated fairly and feel safe from harm. When a person breaks a law, he or she has done something unfair or hurtful. He or she may have to go to jail. But breaking the law doesn't make someone a bad person. It makes him or her a person who made a bad choice.

Laws help people get along with each other. ▶

A Time-Out Place

Your family has rules that everyone has to follow. These rules help everyone get along with each other. If you break a rule, you will face the **consequences** (KON-seh-kwen-sez). Some families have a time-out chair. The child who has broken the rule has to sit in the time-out chair, away from the rest of the family. This gives her time to think about why she broke the rule, and why breaking the rule was wrong. Jail is a time-out place for grown-ups.

◀ A time-out chair gives the person who broke the rules a chance to think about what she did and why she did it.

Life in Jail

Once a person is in jail, he is called a **prisoner** (PRIH-zen-er). Being in jail gives the prisoner a chance to think about why he broke the law. He can decide to change the way he acts so that he doesn't break the law again. Some jails have classes where prisoners can learn new job **skills** (SKILZ) or how to be better parents. Other classes teach prisoners how to give up doing things that hurt them, such as using drugs or alcohol.

Many prisoners use their time in jail to think ▶ about what they did wrong and why.

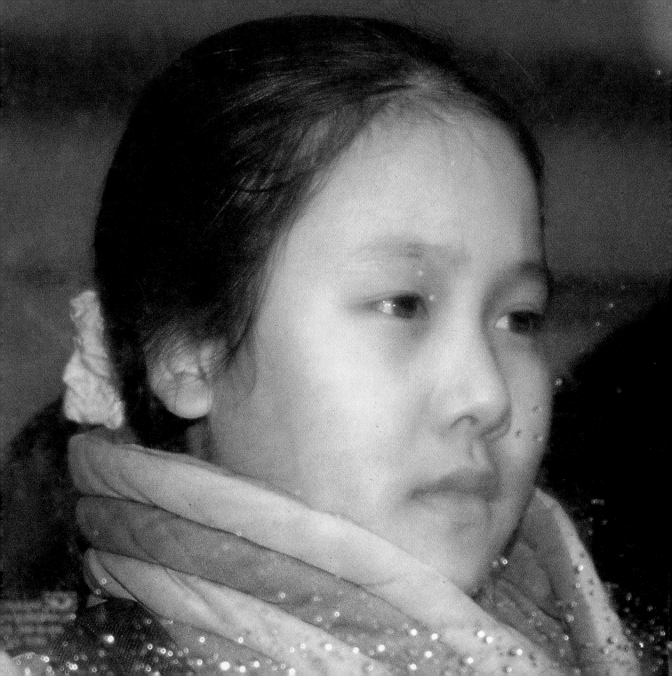

How Long?

Your parent may be in jail for a few months or for many years. The length of time a person is in jail depends on many things. These things include what the person did, if the person has been in jail before, and the way that person acts in jail. There will be changes in your life no matter how long your parent is in jail. But two things will never change. You did not do anything wrong. And the parent in jail still loves and needs you.

◀ It may be hard, but remember that your parent cares about you very much.

Changes Around You

It can be hard on a family when a parent is in jail. It is unfair, but some of your friends, neighbors, and even your **relatives** (REL-uh-tivz) may start to treat you differently. They may stop coming over to visit. They may try to make you feel bad about what your parent did. But it is important to remember that you and your family are not to blame for the bad choices of one parent.

True friends love you no matter what bad choices your parent made. ▶

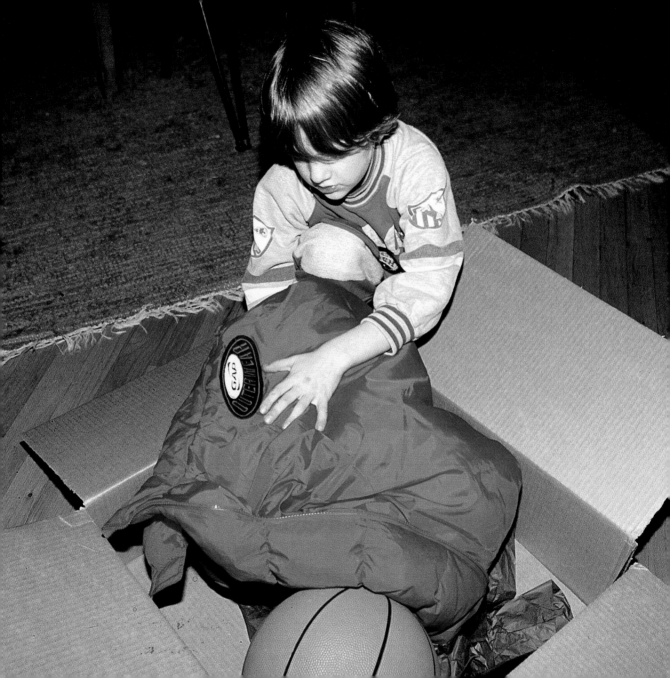

Changes in Your Family

Things will change within your family. With one parent gone, your family may have less money to live on. It will be important for you to help more at home. If you were living with just one parent, and that parent goes to jail, you may have to live with relatives or with a **foster family** (FOHS-ter FAM-ih-lee). This can be a scary time. But know that your family still loves you, and that you will always be taken care of by someone.

◀ One of the changes that you may face is having to move.

17

Keeping in Touch

You will probably miss the parent who's in jail. And your parent will miss you, too. You may be able to visit him or her sometimes. Your other parent, a relative, or another adult can find out if you can visit your parent in jail.

But even if you can't visit your parent, you can keep in touch by writing letters. Your mom or dad will be very happy to hear from you. And he or she can probably write back, too.

One way to keep in touch with your parent in jail is by writing letters. ▶

How Do You Feel?

You may have a lot of confusing feelings about your parent in jail. Someone you love did something wrong. You may feel angry, hurt, sad, ashamed, or **embarrassed** (em-BAYR-est). You may miss your parent. You may even feel guilty about what your parent did. All of these feelings are normal. It is important to remember that *you* did nothing wrong. Talking to your other parent, a teacher, counselor, minister, or rabbi can help you understand and deal with your feelings.

◀ Talking to an adult about what you're feeling can help you learn how to deal with those feelings.

Life After Prison

In most cases, the parent will come home after he or she is **released** (ree-LEEST) from jail. Things will be different once your parent is home. You will need time to get to know your parent again. It may take some time for your parent and your family to feel comfortable with each other. It is important that you and your parent talk openly with each other about how you feel. Your parent made some bad choices in the past. But he or she can help make sure that you make good choices in your life.

Glossary

consequence (KON-seh-kwents) The result of an action.

embarrassed (em-BAYR-est) To feel uneasy or ashamed.

foster family (FOHS-ter FAM-ih-lee) Family who takes care of you when your birth parents can't.

prisoner (PRIH-zen-er) A person who is in jail.

punishment (PUN-ish-ment) The penalty for doing something wrong.

relative (REL-uh-tiv) Person who belongs to the same family that you do.

released (ree-LEEST) To be let go from somewhere.

skill (SKIL) Being able to do something well.

Index